A Heart of Praise

Tena DeGraaf

WESTBOW
PRESS®
A DIVISION OF THOMAS NELSON
& ZONDERVAN

Copyright © 2017 Tena DeGraaf.

All rights reserved. No part of this book may be used or reproduced by any means, graphic, electronic, or mechanical, including photocopying, recording, taping or by any information storage retrieval system without the written permission of the author except in the case of brief quotations embodied in critical articles and reviews.

Scripture taken from Holy Bible, New International Version®, NIV®
Copyright © 1973, 1978, 1984, 2011 by Biblica, Inc®
Used by permission. All rights reserved worldwide.

This book is a work of non-fiction. Unless otherwise noted, the author and the publisher make no explicit guarantees as to the accuracy of the information contained in this book and in some cases, names of people and places have been altered to protect their privacy.

WestBow Press books may be ordered through booksellers or by contacting:

WestBow Press
A Division of Thomas Nelson & Zondervan
1663 Liberty Drive
Bloomington, IN 47403
www.westbowpress.com
1 (866) 928-1240

Because of the dynamic nature of the Internet, any web addresses or links contained in this book may have changed since publication and may no longer be valid. The views expressed in this work are solely those of the author and do not necessarily reflect the views of the publisher, and the publisher hereby disclaims any responsibility for them.

Any people depicted in stock imagery provided by Thinkstock are models, and such images are being used for illustrative purposes only.
Certain stock imagery © Thinkstock.

ISBN: 978-1-5127-5540-4 (sc)
ISBN: 978-1-5127-5541-1 (hc)
ISBN: 978-1-5127-5539-8 (e)

Library of Congress Control Number: 2016914460

Print information available on the last page.

WestBow Press rev. date: 12/28/2016

Acknowledgements

To my heavenly Father who never changes.
May this book bring glory and honor to Your Name.

Introduction

A Heart of Praise was designed to make the most of small fragments of time to reflect on verses that praise the Lord. You may keep this book on your nightstand, the kitchen counter, or in your car. Regardless of where you read it, it will always remind you of the holiness and righteousness of God. There is a daily verse of praise beginning with Exodus in January and ending with Revelation in December. This collection of daily Scriptures and accompanying space for personal journaling will enrich your daily walk with God by providing structure for your own reflection and meditation on God's Word. May this book become as meaningful to you as writing it has been to me. And may you develop a heart of praise as you read it each day.

Tena

January 1

I will sing to the Lord,
for he is highly exalted.
Exodus 15:1

January 2

The Lord is my strength and my defense;
he has become my salvation.
He is my God, and I will praise him,
my father's God, and I will exalt him.
Exodus 15:2

January 3

Who among the gods is like you, Lord?
Who is like you—
majestic in holiness, awesome in glory,
working wonders?
Exodus 15:11

January 4

The LORD reigns
for ever and ever.
Exodus 15:18

January 5

Sovereign LORD, you have begun to show
to your servant your greatness and your
strong hand. For what god is there
in heaven or on earth who can do the
deeds and mighty works you do?
Deuteronomy 3:24

January 6

Acknowledge and take to heart this day that the
LORD is God in heaven above and on the
earth below. There is no other.
Deuteronomy 4:39

January 7

When you have eaten and are satisfied,
praise the LORD your God for the
good land he has given you.
Deuteronomy 8:10

January 8

To the LORD your God belong the heavens,
even the highest heavens, the earth
and everything in it.
Deuteronomy 10:14

January 9

For the LORD your God is God of gods
and Lord of lords,
the great God, mighty and awesome,
who shows no partiality and accepts no bribes.
Deuteronomy 10:17

January 10

He is the one you praise; he is your God,
who performed for you those great and awesome
wonders you saw with your own eyes.
Deuteronomy 10:21

January 11

I will proclaim the name of the LORD.
Oh, praise the greatness of our God!
He is the Rock, his works are perfect,
and all his ways are just. A faithful God who
does no wrong, upright and just is he.
Deuteronomy 32:3–4

January 12

For the LORD your God is God in heaven above
and on the earth below.
Joshua 2:11

January 13

Hear this, you kings! Listen, you rulers!
I, even I, will sing to the Lord;
I will praise the Lord, the God of Israel, in song.
Judges 5:3

January 14

There is no one holy like the Lord;
there is no one besides you;
there is no Rock like our God.
1 Samuel 2:2

January 15

How great you are, Sovereign Lord!
There is no one like you, and there is no
God but you, as we have heard with our own ears.
2 Samuel 7:22

January 16

I called to the LORD, who is worthy of praise,
and have been saved from my enemies.
2 Samuel 22:4

January 17

The LORD lives! Praise be to my Rock!
Exalted be my God, the Rock, my Savior!
2 Samuel 22:47

January 18

Therefore I will praise you, LORD,
among the nations;
I will sing the praises of your name.
2 Samuel 22:50

January 19

LORD, the God of Israel,
there is no God like you
in heaven above or on earth below.
1 Kings 8:23

January 20

Praise be to the LORD, who has given rest to
his people Israel just as he promised.
Not one word has failed of all the good promises
he gave through his servant Moses.
1 Kings 8:56

January 21

The LORD—he is God!
The LORD—he is God!
1 Kings 18:39

January 22

Lord, the God of Israel, enthroned between the cherubim, you alone are God over all the kingdoms of the earth. You have made heaven and earth.
2 Kings 19:15

_____
_____
_____
_____

January 23

Give praise to the Lord, proclaim his name;
make known among the nations what he has done.
Sing to him, sing praise to him; tell of all
his wonderful acts. Glory in his holy name;
let the hearts of those who seek the Lord rejoice.
1 Chronicles 16:8–10

_____
_____
_____
_____

January 24

Sing to the Lord, all the earth; proclaim his salvation day after day. Declare his glory among the nations, his marvelous deeds among all peoples.
1 Chronicles 16:23–24

_____
_____
_____
_____

January 25

For great is the LORD and most worthy of praise;
he is to be feared above all gods.
For all the gods of the nations are idols,
but the LORD made the heavens.
Splendor and majesty are before him;
strength and joy are in his dwelling place.
1 Chronicles 16:25–27

_____
_____
_____
_____

January 26

Ascribe to the LORD, all you families of nations,
ascribe to the LORD glory and strength.
Ascribe to the LORD the glory due his name;
bring an offering and come before him.
Worship the LORD in the splendor of his holiness.
1 Chronicles 16:28–29

_____
_____
_____
_____

January 27

Let the heavens rejoice, let the earth be glad;
let them say among the nations,
"The LORD reigns!"
1 Chronicles 16:31

January 28

Give thanks to the LORD, for he is good;
his love endures forever.
1 Chronicles 16:34

January 29

Praise be to the LORD, the God of Israel,
from everlasting to everlasting.
1 Chronicles 16:36

January 30

There is no one like you, Lord, and there is no God but you, as we have heard with our own ears.
1 Chronicles 17:20

January 31

Praise be to you, Lord,
the God of our father Israel,
from everlasting to everlasting.
Yours, Lord, is the greatness and the power
and the glory and the majesty and the splendor,
for everything in heaven and earth is yours.
Yours, Lord, is the kingdom;
you are exalted as head over all.
Wealth and honor come from you;
you are the ruler of all things.
In your hands are strength and power
to exalt and give strength to all.
Now, our God, we give you thanks,
and praise your glorious name.
1 Chronicles 29:10–13

February 1

The trumpeters and musicians joined in unison
to give praise and thanks to
the Lord. Accompanied by trumpets, cymbals
and other instruments, the singers raised their voices
in praise to the Lord and sang:
"He is good; his love endures forever."
2 Chronicles 5:13

February 2

He is good; his love endures forever.
2 Chronicles 7:3

February 3

Lord, the God of our ancestors, are you not the God
who is in heaven? You rule over all the kingdoms
of the nations. Power and might are in your hand,
and no one can withstand you.
2 Chronicles 20:6

February 4

Give thanks to the LORD, for his love endures forever.
2 Chronicles 20:21

February 5

Blessed be your glorious name,
and may it be exalted above all blessing and praise.
You alone are the LORD. You made the heavens,
even the highest heavens, and all their starry host,
the earth and all that is on it, the seas and all
that is in them. You give life to everything,
and the multitudes of heaven worship you.
Nehemiah 9:5–6

February 6

Naked I came from my mother's womb, and naked
I will depart. The LORD gave and the LORD has
taken away; may the name of the LORD be praised.
Job 1:21

February 7

To God belong wisdom and power;
counsel and understanding are his.

Job 12:13

February 8

God is exalted in his power.
Who is a teacher like him?

Job 36:22

February 9

How great is God—
beyond our understanding!
The number of his years is past finding out.

Job 36:26

February 10

Out of the north he comes in golden splendor;
God comes in awesome majesty.
Job 37:22

February 11

The Almighty is beyond our reach
and exalted in power;
in his justice and great righteousness,
he does not oppress.
Job 37:23

February 12

I know that you can do all things;
no purpose of yours can be thwarted.
Job 42:2

February 13

I will give thanks to the LORD
because of his righteousness;
I will sing the praises of the name of
the LORD Most High.
Psalm 7:17

February 14

When I consider your heavens,
the work of your fingers, the moon and the stars,
which you have set in place,
what is mankind that you are mindful of them,
human beings that you care for them?
Psalm 8:3–4

February 15

LORD, our Lord,
how majestic is your name in all the earth!
Psalm 8:9

February 16

I will give thanks to you, Lord, with all my heart;
I will tell of all your wonderful deeds.
Psalm 9:1

February 17

I will be glad and rejoice in you;
I will sing the praises of your name, O Most High.
Psalm 9:2

February 18

Sing the praises of the Lord, enthroned in Zion;
proclaim among the nations what he has done.
Psalm 9:11

February 19

The LORD is in his holy temple;
the LORD is on his heavenly throne.
Psalm 11:4

February 20

I will sing the LORD's praise,
for he has been good to me.
Psalm 13:6

February 21

I will praise the LORD, who counsels me;
even at night my heart instructs me.
Psalm 16:7

February 22

I love you, Lord, my strength.
Psalm 18:1

February 23

I called to the Lord, who is worthy of praise,
and I have been saved from my enemies.
Psalm 18:3

February 24

The Lord lives! Praise be to my Rock!
Exalted be God my Savior!
Psalm 18:46

February 25

Therefore I will praise you, LORD, among the nations;
I will sing the praises of your name.
Psalm 18:49

February 26

The heavens declare the glory of God;
the skies proclaim the work of his hands.
Psalm 19:1

February 27

May these words of my mouth
and this meditation of my heart
be pleasing in your sight,
LORD, my Rock and my Redeemer.
Psalm 19:14

February 28

Be exalted in your strength, LORD;
we will sing and praise your might.
Psalm 21:13

_____
_____
_____
_____

February 29

I will declare your name to my people;
in the assembly I will praise you.
Psalm 22:22

_____
_____
_____
_____

March 1

All the rich of the earth will feast and worship;
all who go down to the dust will kneel before him—
those who cannot keep themselves alive.
Psalm 22:29

March 2

Who is this King of glory?
The LORD strong and mighty,
the LORD mighty in battle.
Psalm 24:8

March 3

Who is he, this King of glory?
The LORD Almighty—
he is the King of glory.
Psalm 24:10

March 4

I wash my hands in innocence,
and go about your altar, Lord,
proclaiming aloud your praise
and telling of all your wonderful deeds.
Psalm 26:6–7

_____
_____
_____
_____

March 5

My feet stand on level ground;
in the great congregation I will praise the Lord.
Psalm 26:12

_____
_____
_____
_____

March 6

One thing I ask from the Lord, this only do I seek:
that I may dwell in the house of the Lord
all the days of my life, to gaze on the beauty
of the Lord and to seek him in his temple.
Psalm 27:4

_____
_____
_____
_____

March 7

Then my head will be exalted
above the enemies who surround me;
at his sacred tent I will sacrifice with shouts of joy;
I will sing and make music to the LORD.
Psalm 27:6

March 8

Praise be to the LORD,
for he has heard my cry for mercy.
Psalm 28:6

March 9

The LORD is my strength and my shield;
my heart trusts in him, and he helps me.
My heart leaps for joy,
and with my song I praise him.
Psalm 28:7

March 10

Ascribe to the LORD, you heavenly beings,
ascribe to the LORD glory and strength.
Ascribe to the LORD the glory due his name;
worship the LORD in the splendor of his holiness.
Psalm 29:1–2

March 11

The LORD sits enthroned over the flood;
the LORD is enthroned as King forever.
Psalm 29:10

March 12

Sing the praises of the LORD, you his faithful people;
praise his holy name.
Psalm 30:4

March 13

That my heart may sing your praises and not be silent.
Lord my God, I will praise you forever.
Psalm 30:12

March 14

Rejoice in the Lord and be glad, you righteous;
sing, all you who are upright in heart!
Psalm 32:11

March 15

Sing joyfully to the Lord, you righteous;
it is fitting for the upright to praise him.
Psalm 33:1

March 16

Praise the L ORD with the harp;
make music to him on the ten-stringed lyre.
Psalm 33:2

March 17

Sing to him a new song;
play skillfully, and shout for joy.
Psalm 33:3

March 18

I will extol the L ORD at all times;
his praise will always be on my lips.
Psalm 34:1

March 19

I will glory in the LORD;
let the afflicted hear and rejoice.
Psalm 34:2

March 20

Glorify the LORD with me;
let us exalt his name together.
Psalm 34:3

March 21

My whole being will exclaim,
"Who is like you, LORD?
You rescue the poor from those too strong for them,
the poor and needy from those who rob them."
Psalm 35:10

March 22

I will give you thanks in the great assembly;
among the throngs I will praise you.
Psalm 35:18

March 23

My tongue will proclaim your righteousness,
your praises all day long.
Psalm 35:28

March 24

He put a new song in my mouth,
a hymn of praise to our God.
Psalm 40:3

March 25

Many, LORD my God, are the wonders you have done,
the things you planned for us.
None can compare with you;
were I to speak and tell of your deeds,
they would be too many to declare.
Psalm 40:5

March 26

But may all who seek you rejoice and be glad in you;
may those who long for your saving help always say,
"The LORD is great!"
Psalm 40:16

March 27

Praise be to the LORD, the God of Israel,
from everlasting to everlasting. Amen and Amen.
Psalm 41:13

March 28

As the deer pants for streams of water,
so my soul pants for you, my God.
My soul thirsts for God, for the living God.
When can I go and meet with God?
Psalm 42:1–2

March 29

Why, my soul, are you downcast?
Why so disturbed within me?
Put your hope in God, for I will yet praise him,
my Savior and my God.
Psalm 42:5

March 30

Then I will go to the altar of God,
to God, my joy and my delight.
I will praise you with the lyre, O God, my God.
Psalm 43:4

March 31

In God we make our boast all day long,
and we will praise your name forever.
Psalm 44:8

April 1

I will perpetuate your memory through all
generations; therefore the nations will
praise you for ever and ever.
Psalm 45:17

April 2

Be still, and know that I am God;
I will be exalted among the nations,
I will be exalted in the earth.
Psalm 46:10

April 3

For the Lord Most High is awesome,
the great King over all the earth.
Psalm 47:2

April 4

Sing praises to God, sing praises;
sing praises to our King, sing praises.
Psalm 47:6

April 5

For God is the King of all the earth;
sing to him a psalm of praise.
Psalm 47:7

April 6

God reigns over the nations;
God is seated on his holy throne.
Psalm 47:8

April 7

Great is the LORD, and most worthy of praise,
in the city of our God, his holy mountain.
Psalm 48:1

April 8

Open my lips, Lord,
and my mouth will declare your praise.
Psalm 51:15

April 9

For what you have done I will always praise you
in the presence of your faithful people.
And I will hope in your name,
for your name is good.
Psalm 52:9

April 10

I will sacrifice a freewill offering to you;
I will praise your name, LORD, for it is good.
Psalm 54:6

April 11

In God, whose word I praise—
in God I trust and am not afraid.
What can mere mortals do to me?
Psalm 56:4

April 12

Be exalted, O God, above the heavens;
let your glory be over all the earth.
Psalm 57:5

April 13

My heart, O God, is steadfast,
my heart is steadfast; I will sing and make music.
Psalm 57:7

April 14

I will praise you, Lord, among the nations;
I will sing of you among the peoples.
For great is your love, reaching to the heavens;
your faithfulness reaches to the skies.
Psalm 57:9–10

April 15

But I will sing of your strength,
in the morning I will sing of your love;
for you are my fortress, my refuge in times of trouble.
Psalm 59:16

April 16

You are my strength, I sing praise to you;
you, God, are my fortress, my God on whom I can rely.
Psalm 59:17

April 17

Then I will ever sing in praise of your name
and fulfill my vows day after day.
Psalm 61:8

April 18

You, God, are my God,
earnestly I seek you; I thirst for you,
my whole being longs for you,
in a dry and parched land
where there is no water.
Psalm 63:1

April 19

Because your love is better than life,
my lips will glorify you.
Psalm 63:3

April 20

I will praise you as long as I live,
and in your name I will lift up my hands.
Psalm 63:4

April 21

I will be fully satisfied as with the richest of foods;
with singing lips my mouth will praise you.
Psalm 63:5

April 22

The righteous will rejoice in the LORD
and take refuge in him;
all the upright in heart will glory in him!
Psalm 64:10

April 23

Shout for joy to God, all the earth!
Psalm 66:1

April 24

Sing the glory of his name;
make his praise glorious.
Psalm 66:2

April 25

Say to God, "How awesome are your deeds!
So great is your power
that your enemies cringe before you.
All the earth bows down to you;
they sing praise to you,
they sing the praises of your name."
Psalm 66:3–4

April 26

Praise our God, all peoples,
let the sound of his praise be heard.
Psalm 66:8

April 27

I cried out to him with my mouth;
his praise was on my tongue.
Psalm 66:17

April 28

Praise be to God,
who has not rejected my prayer
or withheld his love from me!
Psalm 66:20

April 29

May the peoples praise you, God;
may all the peoples praise you.
Psalm 67:3

April 30

Sing to God, sing in praise of his name,
extol him who rides on the clouds;
rejoice before him—
his name is the Lord.
Psalm 68:4

May 1

Praise be to the Lord, to God our Savior,
who daily bears our burdens.
Psalm 68:19

May 2

Praise God in the great congregation;
praise the Lord in the assembly of Israel.
Psalm 68:26

May 3

Sing to God, you kingdoms of the earth,
sing praise to the Lord.
Psalm 68:32

May 4

Proclaim the power of God,
whose majesty is over Israel,
whose power is in the heavens.
Psalm 68:34

May 5

You, God, are awesome in your sanctuary;
the God of Israel gives
power and strength to his people.
Praise be to God!
Psalm 68:35

May 6

I will praise God's name in song
and glorify him with thanksgiving.
Psalm 69:30

May 7

Let heaven and earth praise him,
the seas and all that move in them.
Psalm 69:34

May 8

But may all who seek you
rejoice and be glad in you;
may those who long for your saving help always say,
"The LORD is great!"
Psalm 70:4

May 9

From birth I have relied on you;
you brought me forth from my mother's womb.
I will ever praise you.
Psalm 71:6

May 10

My mouth is filled with your praise,
declaring your splendor all day long.
Psalm 71:8

May 11

As for me, I will always have hope;
I will praise you more and more.
Psalm 71:14

May 12

My mouth will tell of your righteous deeds,
of your saving acts all day long—
though I know not how to relate them all.
Psalm 71:15

May 13

I will come and proclaim your mighty acts,
Sovereign Lord;
I will proclaim your righteous deeds, yours alone.
Psalm 71:16

May 14

Since my youth, God, you have taught me,
and to this day I declare your marvelous deeds.
Psalm 71:17

May 15

Your righteousness, God, reaches to the heavens,
you who have done great things.
Who is like you, God?
Psalm 71:19

May 16

I will praise you with the harp
for your faithfulness, my God;
I will sing praise to you with the lyre,
Holy One of Israel.
Psalm 71:22

May 17

My lips will shout for joy
when I sing praise to you—
I whom you have delivered.
Psalm 71:23

May 18

Praise be to the Lord God, the God of Israel,
who alone does marvelous deeds.
Psalm 72:18

May 19

Praise be to his glorious name forever;
may the whole earth be filled with his glory.
Amen and Amen.
Psalm 72:19

May 20

Whom have I in heaven but you?
And earth has nothing I desire besides you.
Psalm 73:25

May 21

But as for me, it is good to be near God.
I have made the Sovereign LORD my refuge;
I will tell of all your deeds.
Psalm 73:28

May 22

Do not let the oppressed retreat in disgrace;
may the poor and needy praise your name.
Psalm 74:21

May 23

We praise you, God,
we praise you, for your Name is near;
people tell of your wonderful deeds.
Psalm 75:1

May 24

As for me, I will declare this forever;
I will sing praise to the God of Jacob.
Psalm 75:9

May 25

You are radiant with light,
more majestic than mountains rich with game.
Psalm 76:4

_____
_____
_____
_____

May 26

Your ways, God, are holy.
What god is as great as our God?
Psalm 77:13

_____
_____
_____
_____

May 27

We will not hide them from their descendants;
we will tell the next generation
the praiseworthy deeds of the LORD,
his power, and the wonders he has done.
Psalm 78:4

_____
_____
_____
_____

May 28

Then we your people, the sheep of your pasture,
will praise you forever;
from generation to generation
we will proclaim your praise.
Psalm 79:13

May 29

Sing for joy to God our strength;
shout aloud to the God of Jacob!
Psalm 81:1

May 30

Let them know that you,
whose name is the Lord—
that you alone are the
Most High over all the earth.
Psalm 83:18

May 31

How lovely is your dwelling place,
Lord Almighty!
My soul yearns, even faints,
for the courts of the Lord;
my heart and my flesh cry out
for the living God.
Psalm 84:1–2

_____
_____
_____
_____

June 1

Blessed are those who dwell in your house;
they are ever praising you.
Psalm 84:4

June 2

All the nations you have made
will come and worship before you, Lord;
they will bring glory to your name.
For you are great and do marvelous deeds;
you alone are God.
Psalm 86:9–10

June 3

I will praise you, Lord my God,
with all my heart;
I will glorify your name forever.
Psalm 86:12

June 4

I will sing of the LORD's great love forever;
with my mouth I will make your faithfulness
known through all generations.
Psalm 89:1

June 5

I will declare that your love stands firm forever,
that you have established your faithfulness
in heaven itself.
Psalm 89:2

June 6

The heavens praise your wonders, LORD,
your faithfulness too,
in the assembly of the holy ones.
Psalm 89:5

June 7

For who in the skies above
can compare with the Lord?
Who is like the Lord
among the heavenly beings?
Psalm 89:6

June 8

Who is like you, Lord God Almighty?
You, Lord, are mighty,
and your faithfulness surrounds you.
Psalm 89:8

June 9

Praise be to the Lord forever!
Amen and Amen.
Psalm 89:52

June 10

It is good to praise the LORD
and make music to your name, O Most High,
proclaiming your love in the morning
and your faithfulness at night.
Psalm 92:1–2

June 11

For you make me glad by your deeds, LORD;
I sing for joy at what your hands have done.
Psalm 92:4

June 12

How great are your works, LORD,
how profound your thoughts!
Psalm 92:5

June 13

But you, LORD, are forever exalted.
Psalm 92:8

June 14

The LORD is upright;
he is my Rock,
and there is no wickedness in him.
Psalm 92:15

June 15

The LORD reigns, he is robed in majesty;
the LORD is robed in majesty
and armed with strength.
Psalm 93:1

June 16

Mightier than the thunder of the great waters,
mightier than the breakers of the sea—
the LORD on high is mighty.
Psalm 93:4

June 17

Come, let us sing for joy to the LORD;
let us shout aloud to the Rock of our salvation.
Psalm 95:1

June 18

Let us come before him with thanksgiving
and extol him with music and song.
Psalm 95:2

June 19

For the LORD is the great God,
the great King above all gods.
Psalm 95:3

June 20

In his hand are the depths of the earth,
and the mountain peaks belong to him.
The sea is his, for he made it,
and his hands formed the dry land.
Psalm 95:4–5

June 21

Come, let us bow down in worship,
let us kneel before the LORD our Maker.
Psalm 95:6

June 22

Sing to the Lord a new song;
sing to the Lord, all the earth.
Psalm 96:1

June 23

Sing to the Lord, praise his name;
proclaim his salvation day after day.
Psalm 96:2

June 24

Declare his glory among the nations,
his marvelous deeds among all peoples.
Psalm 96:3

June 25

For great is the Lord and most worthy of praise;
he is to be feared above all gods.
Psalm 96:4

June 26

Splendor and majesty are before him;
strength and glory are in his sanctuary.
Psalm 96:6

June 27

Ascribe to the Lord, all you families of nations,
ascribe to the Lord glory and strength.
Psalm 96:7

June 28

Ascribe to the LORD the glory due his name;
bring an offering and come into his courts.
Psalm 96:8

June 29

Worship the LORD in the splendor of his holiness;
tremble before him, all the earth.
Psalm 96:9

June 30

Say among the nations, "The LORD reigns."
The world is firmly established,
it cannot be moved;
he will judge the peoples with equity.
Psalm 96:10

July 1

The LORD reigns, let the earth be glad;
let the distant shores rejoice.

Psalm 97:1

July 2

The heavens proclaim his righteousness,
and all peoples see his glory.

Psalm 97:6

July 3

For you, LORD, are the Most High
over all the earth;
you are exalted far above all gods.

Psalm 97:9

July 4

Rejoice in the LORD, you who are righteous,
and praise his holy name.
Psalm 97:12

July 5

Sing to the LORD a new song,
for he has done marvelous things;
his right hand and his holy arm
have worked salvation for him.
Psalm 98:1

July 6

Shout for joy to the LORD, all the earth,
burst into jubilant song with music.
Psalm 98:4

July 7

Great is the LORD in Zion;
he is exalted over all the nations.
Psalm 99:2

July 8

Let them praise your great and awesome name—
he is holy.
Psalm 99:3

July 9

Exalt the LORD our God
and worship at his footstool;
he is holy.
Psalm 99:5

July 10

Exalt the LORD our God
and worship at his holy mountain,
for the LORD our God is holy.
Psalm 99:9

July 11

Shout for joy to the LORD, all the earth.
Psalm 100:1

July 12

Worship the LORD with gladness;
come before him with joyful songs.
Psalm 100:2

July 13

Enter his gates with thanksgiving
and his courts with praise;
give thanks to him and praise his name.
Psalm 100:4

July 14

I will sing of your love and justice;
to you, Lord, I will sing praise.
Psalm 101:1

July 15

But you, Lord, sit enthroned forever;
your renown endures through all generations.
Psalm 102:12

July 16

Praise the LORD, my soul;
all my inmost being, praise his holy name.
Psalm 103:1

July 17

Praise the LORD, my soul,
and forget not all his benefits.
Psalm 103:2

July 18

Praise the LORD, you his angels,
you mighty ones who do his bidding,
who obey his word.
Praise the LORD, all his heavenly hosts,
you his servants who do his will.
Psalm 103:20–21

July 19

Praise the LORD, all his works
everywhere in his dominion.
Praise the LORD, my soul.
Psalm 103:22

July 20

Praise the LORD, my soul.
LORD my God, you are very great;
you are clothed with splendor and majesty.
Psalm 104:1

July 21

May the glory of the LORD endure forever;
may the LORD rejoice in his works.
Psalm 104:31

July 22

I will sing to the LORD all my life;
I will sing praise to my God as long as I live.
Psalm 104:33

July 23

May my meditation be pleasing to him,
as I rejoice in the LORD.
Psalm 104:34

July 24

Give praise to the LORD, proclaim his name;
make known among the nations what he has done.
Psalm 105:1

July 25

Sing to him, sing praise to him;
tell of all his wonderful acts.
Psalm 105:2

July 26

Glory in his holy name;
let the hearts of those who seek the Lord rejoice.
Psalm 105:3

July 27

Praise the Lord.
Give thanks to the Lord, for he is good;
his love endures forever.
Psalm 106:1

July 28

Who can proclaim the mighty acts of the Lord
or fully declare his praise?
Psalm 106:2

July 29

Praise be to the Lord, the God of Israel,
from everlasting to everlasting.
Let all the people say, "Amen!"
Praise the Lord.
Psalm 106:48

July 30

Let them give thanks to the Lord
for his unfailing love
and his wonderful deeds for mankind.
Psalm 107:8

July 31

Let them give thanks to the LORD
for his unfailing love
and his wonderful deeds for mankind.
Let them sacrifice thank offerings
and tell of his works with songs of joy.
Psalm 107:21–22

_____
_____
_____
_____

August 1

Let them exalt him in the assembly of the people
and praise him in the council of the elders.
Psalm 107:32

August 2

My heart, O God, is steadfast;
I will sing and make music with all my soul.
Psalm 108:1

August 3

I will praise you, Lord, among the nations;
I will sing of you among the peoples.
Psalm 108:3

August 4

For great is your love, higher than the heavens;
your faithfulness reaches to the skies.
Psalm 108:4

August 5

Be exalted, O God, above the heavens;
let your glory be over all the earth.
Psalm 108:5

August 6

With my mouth I will greatly extol the Lord;
in the great throng of worshipers I will praise him.
Psalm 109:30

August 7

Praise the LORD.
I will extol the LORD with all my heart
in the council of the upright and in the assembly.
Psalm 111:1

August 8

Great are the works of the LORD;
they are pondered by all who delight in them.
Psalm 111:2

August 9

Glorious and majestic are his deeds,
and his righteousness endures forever.
Psalm 111:3

August 10

He provided redemption for his people;
he ordained his covenant forever—
holy and awesome is his name.

Psalm 111:9

August 11

The fear of the LORD is the beginning of wisdom;
all who follow his precepts
have good understanding.
To him belongs eternal praise.

Psalm 111:10

August 12

Praise the LORD.
Praise the LORD, you his servants;
praise the name of the LORD.

Psalm 113:1

August 13

Let the name of the LORD be praised,
both now and forevermore.
Psalm 113:2

August 14

From the rising of the sun
to the place where it sets,
the name of the LORD is to be praised.
Psalm 113:3

August 15

The LORD is exalted over all the nations,
his glory above the heavens.
Psalm 113:4

August 16

Who is like the LORD our God,
the One who sits enthroned on high,
who stoops down to look
on the heavens and the earth?
Psalm 113:5–6

August 17

Not to us, LORD, not to us
but to your name be the glory,
because of your love and faithfulness.
Psalm 115:1

August 18

Praise the LORD, all you nations;
extol him, all you peoples.
Psalm 117:1

August 19

For great is his love toward us,
and the faithfulness of the Lord endures forever.
Praise the Lord.
Psalm 117:2

August 20

Give thanks to the Lord, for he is good;
his love endures forever.
Psalm 118:1

August 21

The Lord has done it this very day;
let us rejoice today and be glad.
Psalm 118:24

August 22

You are my God, and I will praise you;
you are my God, and I will exalt you.
Psalm 118:28

August 23

I will praise you with an upright heart
as I learn your righteous laws.
Psalm 119:7

August 24

Praise be to you, Lord;
teach me your decrees.
Psalm 119:12

August 25

Accept, Lord,
the willing praise of my mouth,
and teach me your laws.
Psalm 119:108

August 26

Seven times a day I praise you
for your righteous laws.
Psalm 119:164

August 27

May my lips overflow with praise,
for you teach me your decrees.
Psalm 119:171

August 28

Let me live that I may praise you,
and may your laws sustain me.
Psalm 119:175

August 29

I lift up my eyes to you,
to you who sit enthroned in heaven.
Psalm 123:1

August 30

Lift up your hands in the sanctuary
and praise the LORD.
Psalm 134:2

August 31

Praise the LORD.
Praise the name of the LORD;
praise him, you servants of the LORD,
you who minister in the house of the LORD,
in the courts of the house of our God.
Psalm 135:1–2

September 1

Praise the Lord, for the Lord is good;
sing praise to his name, for that is pleasant.
Psalm 135:3

September 2

I know that the Lord is great,
that our Lord is greater than all gods.
Psalm 135:5

September 3

Your name, Lord, endures forever,
your renown, Lord, through all generations.
Psalm 135:13

September 4

I will praise you, Lord, with all my heart;
before the "gods" I will sing your praise.
Psalm 138:1

___

September 5

I will bow down toward your holy temple
and will praise your name
for your unfailing love and your faithfulness,
for you have so exalted your solemn decree
that it surpasses your fame.
Psalm 138:2

___

September 6

May all the kings of the earth praise you, Lord,
when they hear what you have decreed.
Psalm 138:4

September 7

May they sing of the ways of the LORD,
for the glory of the LORD is great.
Psalm 138:5

September 8

I praise you because I am fearfully
and wonderfully made;
your works are wonderful,
I know that full well.
Psalm 139:14

September 9

May my prayer be set before you like incense;
may the lifting up of my hands be like
the evening sacrifice.
Psalm 141:2

September 10

I remember the days of long ago;
I meditate on all your works
and consider what your hands have done.
Psalm 143:5

September 11

I will sing a new song to you, my God;
on the ten-stringed lyre I will make music to you.
Psalm 144:9

September 12

I will exalt you, my God the King;
I will praise your name for ever and ever.
Psalm 145:1

September 13

Every day I will praise you
and extol your name for ever and ever.
Psalm 145:2

September 14

Great is the LORD and most worthy of praise;
his greatness no one can fathom.
Psalm 145:3

September 15

One generation commends
your works to another;
they tell of your mighty acts.
Psalm 145:4

September 16

They speak of the glorious splendor
of your majesty—
and I will meditate on your wonderful works.
Psalm 145:5

September 17

They tell of the power of
your awesome works—
and I will proclaim your great deeds.
Psalm 145:6

September 18

They celebrate your abundant goodness
and joyfully sing of your righteousness.
Psalm 145:7

September 19

All your works praise you, LORD;
your faithful people extol you.
Psalm 145:10

_____
_____
_____
_____

September 20

They tell of the glory of your kingdom
and speak of your might,
so that all people may know of your mighty acts
and the glorious splendor of your kingdom.
Psalm 145:11–12

_____
_____
_____
_____

September 21

My mouth will speak in praise of the LORD.
Let every creature praise his holy name
for ever and ever.
Psalm 145:21

_____
_____
_____
_____

September 22

Praise the Lord.
Praise the Lord, my soul.
I will praise the Lord all my life;
I will sing praise to my God as long as I live.
Psalm 146:1–2

_____
_____
_____
_____

September 23

The Lord reigns forever,
your God, O Zion, for all generations.
Praise the Lord.
Psalm 146:10

_____
_____
_____
_____

September 24

Praise the Lord.
How good it is to sing praises to our God,
how pleasant and fitting to praise him!
Psalm 147:1

_____
_____
_____
_____

September 25

Great is our Lord and mighty in power;
his understanding has no limit.
Psalm 147:5

September 26

Sing to the LORD with grateful praise;
make music to our God on the harp.
Psalm 147:7

September 27

Praise the LORD.
Praise the LORD from the heavens;
praise him in the heights above.
Psalm 148:1

September 28

Praise him, all his angels;
praise him, all his heavenly hosts.
Psalm 148:2

September 29

Praise him, sun and moon;
praise him, all you shining stars.
Psalm 148:3

September 30

Praise him, you highest heavens
and you waters above the skies.
Psalm 148:4

October 1

Let them praise the name of the Lord,
for at his command they were created.
Psalm 148:5

_____
_____
_____
_____

October 2

Let them praise the name of the Lord,
for his name alone is exalted;
his splendor is above the earth and the heavens.
Psalm 148:13

_____
_____
_____
_____

October 3

Praise the Lord.
Sing to the Lord a new song,
his praise in the assembly of his faithful people.
Psalm 149:1

_____
_____
_____
_____

October 4

Let them praise his name with dancing
and make music to him
with timbrel and harp.
Psalm 149:3

October 5

Praise the Lord.
Praise God in his sanctuary;
praise him in his mighty heavens.
Psalm 150:1

October 6

Praise him for his acts of power;
praise him for his surpassing greatness.
Psalm 150:2

October 7

Praise him with the sounding of the trumpet,
praise him with the harp and lyre.
Psalm 150:3

October 8

Praise him with timbrel and dancing,
praise him with the strings and pipe.
Psalm 150:4

October 9

Praise him with the clash of cymbals,
praise him with resounding cymbals.
Psalm 150:5

October 10

Let everything that has breath praise the LORD.
Praise the LORD.
Psalm 150:6

October 11

Holy, holy, holy is the LORD Almighty;
the whole earth is full of his glory.
Isaiah 6:3

October 12

For to us a child is born, to us a son is given,
and the government will be on his shoulders.
And he will be called
Wonderful Counselor, Mighty God,
Everlasting Father, Prince of Peace.
Isaiah 9:6

October 13

Give praise to the LORD, proclaim his name;
make known among the nations what he
has done, and proclaim that his name is exalted.
Isaiah 12:4

October 14

Sing to the LORD,
for he has done glorious things;
let this be known to all the world.
Isaiah 12:5

October 15

LORD, you are my God;
I will exalt you and praise your name,
for in perfect faithfulness you have done
wonderful things, things planned long ago.
Isaiah 25:1

October 16

The living, the living—
they praise you, as I am doing today;
parents tell their children about your faithfulness.
Isaiah 38:19

October 17

Lift up your eyes and look to the heavens:
Who created all these?
He who brings out the starry host one by one
and calls forth each of them by name.
Because of his great power and mighty strength,
not one of them is missing.
Isaiah 40:26

October 18

Sing to the LORD a new song,
his praise from the ends of the earth,
you who go down to the sea, and all that is in it,
you islands, and all who live in them.
Isaiah 42:10

October 19

Let them give glory to the LORD
and proclaim his praise in the islands.
Isaiah 42:12

October 20

The people I formed for myself
that they may proclaim my praise.
Isaiah 43:21

October 21

Shout for joy, you heavens; rejoice, you earth;
burst into song, you mountains!
For the LORD comforts his people
and will have compassion on his afflicted ones.
Isaiah 49:13

October 22

I will tell of the kindnesses of the LORD,
the deeds for which he is to be praised,
according to all the LORD has done for us—
yes, the many good things he has done
for Israel, according to his
compassion and many kindnesses.
Isaiah 63:7

October 23

No one is like you, LORD; you are great,
and your name is mighty in power.
Jeremiah 10:6

October 24

Who should not fear you,
King of the nations? This is your due.
Among all the wise leaders of the nations and
in all their kingdoms, there is no one like you.
Jeremiah 10:7

October 25

But the LORD is the true God;
he is the living God, the eternal King.
When he is angry, the earth trembles;
the nations cannot endure his wrath.
Jeremiah 10:10

October 26

Heal me, LORD, and I will be healed;
save me and I will be saved,
for you are the one I praise.
Jeremiah 17:14

October 27

Sing to the LORD! Give praise to the LORD!
He rescues the life of the needy
from the hands of the wicked.
Jeremiah 20:13

_____
_____
_____
_____

October 28

Ah, Sovereign LORD, you have made the
heavens and the earth by your great
power and outstretched arm.
Nothing is too hard for you.
Jeremiah 32:17

_____
_____
_____
_____

October 29

Great and mighty God, whose name is the
LORD Almighty, great are your purposes
and mighty are your deeds.
Jeremiah 32:18–19

_____
_____
_____
_____

October 30

Give thanks to the Lord Almighty,
for the Lord is good; his love endures forever.
Jeremiah 33:11

October 31

Yet this I call to mind and therefore I have hope:
Because of the Lord's great love we are
not consumed, for his compassions never fail.
They are new every morning;
great is your faithfulness.
Lamentations 3:21–23

November 1

You, LORD, reign forever;
your throne endures
from generation to generation.
Lamentations 5:19

November 2

The glory of the LORD rose from the place
where it was standing.
Ezekiel 3:12

November 3

Praise be to the name of God for ever and ever;
wisdom and power are his.
Daniel 2:20

November 4

I thank and praise you, God of my ancestors.
Daniel 2:23

November 5

How great are his signs,
how mighty his wonders!
His kingdom is an eternal kingdom;
his dominion endures
from generation to generation.
Daniel 4:3

November 6

His dominion is an eternal dominion;
his kingdom endures
from generation to generation.
Daniel 4:34

November 7

For he is the living God and he endures forever;
his kingdom will not be destroyed,
his dominion will never end.
Daniel 6:26

November 8

He who forms the mountains, who creates the wind,
and who reveals his thoughts to mankind,
who turns dawn to darkness,
and treads on the heights of the earth–
the Lord God Almighty is his name.
Amos 4:13

November 9

But I, with shouts of grateful praise,
will sacrifice to you.
Jonah 2:9

November 10

Yet I will rejoice in the L ORD,
I will be joyful in God my Savior.
Habakkuk 3:18

November 11

Worship the Lord your God,
and serve him only.
Matthew 4:10

November 12

In the same way, let your light shine before others, that they may see your good deeds and glorify your Father in heaven.
Matthew 5:16

November 13

Our Father in heaven,
hallowed be your name,
your kingdom come, your will be done,
on earth as it is in heaven.
Matthew 6:9–10

November 14

My soul glorifies the Lord
and my spirit rejoices in God my Savior.
Luke 1:46–47

November 15

For the Mighty One has done
great things for me—
holy is his name.
Luke 1:49

November 16

Praise be to the Lord, the God of Israel,
because he has come to his people and redeemed them.
Luke 1:68

November 17

Glory to God in the highest heaven,
and on earth peace to those on whom his favor rests.
Luke 2:14

November 18

Yet a time is coming
and has now come when the true
worshipers will worship the Father in the Spirit
and in truth, for they are the kind of
worshipers the Father seeks.
John 4:23

November 19

God is spirit, and his worshipers must worship
in the Spirit and in truth.
John 4:24

November 20

"Hosanna!"
"Blessed is he who comes in the name of the Lord!"
"Blessed is the king of Israel!"
John 12:13

November 21

For since the creation of the world God's
invisible qualities—
his eternal power and divine nature—
have been clearly seen,
being understood from what has been made,
so that people are without excuse.
Romans 1:20

November 22

They exchanged the truth about God for a lie,
and worshiped and served created things rather
than the Creator—
who is forever praised. Amen.
Romans 1:25

_____
_____
_____
_____

November 23

Oh, the depth of the riches of the
wisdom and knowledge of God!
How unsearchable his judgments,
and his paths beyond tracing out!
"Who has known the mind of the Lord?
Or who has been his counselor?"
"Who has ever given to God,
that God should repay them?"
For from him and through him
and for him are all things.
To him be the glory forever! Amen.
Romans 11:33–36

_____
_____
_____
_____

November 24

Therefore, I urge you, brothers and sisters,
in view of God's mercy,
to offer your bodies as a living sacrifice,
holy and pleasing to God—
this is your true and proper worship.
Romans 12:1

November 25

Therefore I will praise you among the Gentiles;
I will sing the praises of your name.
Romans 15:9

November 26

Praise the Lord, all you Gentiles;
let all the peoples extol him.
Romans 15:11

November 27

To the only wise God be glory forever through
Jesus Christ! Amen.
Romans 16:27

November 28

Yet for us there is but one God, the Father,
from whom all things came and for whom
we live; and there is but one Lord,
Jesus Christ, through whom all things came
and through whom we live.
1 Corinthians 8:6

November 29

So whether you eat or drink or whatever you do,
do it all for the glory of God.
1 Corinthians 10:31

November 30

But thanks be to God!
He gives us the victory
through our Lord Jesus Christ.
1 Corinthians 15:57

_____
_____
_____
_____

December 1

Praise be to the God and Father
of our Lord Jesus Christ,
the Father of compassion
and the God of all comfort,
who comforts us in all our troubles,
so that we can comfort
those in any trouble with the comfort
we ourselves receive from God.
2 Corinthians 1:3–4

_____

December 2

Grace and peace to you from God our Father
and the Lord Jesus Christ,
who gave himself for our sins
to rescue us from the present evil age,
according to the will of our God and Father,
to whom be glory for ever and ever. Amen.
Galatians 1:3–5

December 3

Praise be to the God and Father
of our Lord Jesus Christ,
who has blessed us in the heavenly realms
with every spiritual blessing in Christ.
Ephesians 1:3

December 4

To the praise of his glorious grace,
which he has freely given us in the One he loves.
Ephesians 1:6

December 5

Now to him who is able to do immeasurably
more than all we ask or imagine, according
to his power that is at work within us, to him be
glory in the church and in Christ Jesus throughout
all generations, for ever and ever! Amen.
Ephesians 3:20–21

December 6

Speaking to one another with psalms, hymns,
and songs from the Spirit. Sing and make music from
your heart to the Lord, always giving thanks
to God the Father for everything,
in the name of our Lord Jesus Christ.
Ephesians 5:19–20

_____
_____
_____
_____

December 7

Therefore God exalted him to the
highest place and gave him the name
that is above every name,
that at the name of Jesus every knee
should bow, in heaven and on earth
and under the earth, and every tongue
acknowledge that Jesus Christ is Lord,
to the glory of God the Father.
Philippians 2:9–11

_____
_____
_____
_____

December 8

To our God and Father be glory for ever and ever.
Amen.
Philippians 4:20

December 9

Let the message of Christ dwell among you richly
as you teach and admonish one another
with all wisdom through psalms,
hymns, and songs from the Spirit,
singing to God with gratitude in your hearts.
Colossians 3:16

December 10

Now to the King eternal, immortal, invisible,
the only God,
be honor and glory for ever and ever. Amen.
1 Timothy 1:17

December 11

God, the blessed and only Ruler,
the King of kings and Lord of lords, who alone
is immortal and who lives in unapproachable
light, whom no one has seen or can see.
To him be honor and might forever. Amen.
1 Timothy 6:15–16

December 12

I will declare your name to my brothers and sisters;
in the assembly I will sing your praises.
Hebrews 2:12

December 13

Therefore, since we are receiving a kingdom that
cannot be shaken, let us be thankful, and so
worship God acceptably with reverence and awe,
for our "God is a consuming fire."
Hebrews 12:28–29

December 14

Through Jesus, therefore, let us continually
offer to God a sacrifice of praise—
the fruit of lips that openly profess his name.
Hebrews 13:15

_____
_____
_____
_____

December 15

With the tongue we praise our Lord and Father.
James 3:9

_____
_____
_____
_____

December 16

But you are a chosen people,
a royal priesthood, a holy nation,
God's special possession, that you may declare
the praises of him who called you out of
darkness into his wonderful light.
1 Peter 2:9

_____
_____
_____
_____

December 17

If anyone speaks, they should do so as one who speaks
the very words of God. If anyone serves,
they should do so with the strength God provides,
so that in all things God may be praised
through Jesus Christ.
To him be the glory and the power
for ever and ever. Amen.
1 Peter 4:11

December 18

And the God of all grace,
who called you to his eternal glory
in Christ, after you have suffered a little while,
will himself restore you
and make you strong, firm and steadfast.
To him be the power for ever and ever. Amen.
1 Peter 5:10–11

December 19

But grow in the grace and knowledge of our
Lord and Savior Jesus Christ.
To him be glory both now and forever! Amen.
2 Peter 3:18

December 20

To the only God our Savior be glory, majesty,
power and authority, through Jesus Christ our Lord,
before all ages, now and forevermore! Amen.
Jude 1:25

December 21

To him who loves us and has freed us from our
sins by his blood, and has made us to be a
kingdom and priests to serve his God and Father—
to him be glory and power for ever and ever!
Amen.
Revelation 1:5–6

December 22

Holy, holy, holy is the Lord God Almighty,
who was, and is, and is to come.
Revelation 4:8

December 23

You are worthy, our Lord and God,
to receive glory and honor and power,
for you created all things, and by your will
they were created and have their being.
Revelation 4:11

December 24

Worthy is the Lamb, who was slain,
to receive power and wealth and wisdom
and strength and honor and glory and praise!
Revelation 5:12

December 25

To him who sits on the throne and to the Lamb
be praise and honor and glory and power,
for ever and ever!
Revelation 5:13

December 26

Amen! Praise and glory
and wisdom and thanks and honor
and power and strength
be to our God for ever and ever. Amen!
Revelation 7:12

December 27

We give thanks to you, Lord God Almighty,
the One who is and who was,
because you have taken your great power
and have begun to reign.
Revelation 11:17

December 28

Great and marvelous are your deeds,
Lord God Almighty.
Just and true are your ways, King of the nations.
Revelation 15:3

December 29

Who will not fear you, Lord,
and bring glory to your name?
For you alone are holy.
All nations will come and worship before you,
for your righteous acts have been revealed.
Revelation 15:4

December 30

Hallelujah!
Salvation and glory and power belong to our God.
Revelation 19:1

December 31

Hallelujah!
For our Lord God Almighty reigns.
Let us rejoice and be glad
and give him glory!
Revelation 19:6–7

About the Author

As a speaker, teacher, and author, Tena's passion is to encourage women to grow in faith, hope, and love.
She and her family make their home in Illinois.
To learn more about Tena's speaking and writing, visit tenadegraaf.com.

Printed in the United States
By Bookmasters